THIS IS WHAT I'VE BEEN TOLD

MII YI GAA-BI-WIINDMAAGOOYANG

Written & Illustrated by
Juliana Armstrong

I've been told that our ancestors have carried our language and culture since time immemorial; that they walk beside us on our journey through this physical realm. Our Creation story and our language share our worldview through many great teachings and leave us with many great teachers.

Gookmis *(Go•k•miss)* — Grandmother

Gookmis is a special teacher in our lives. She is a storyteller and knowledge keeper who shares her experiences and teachings with all who will listen.

"Gookmis, why do you share your teachings with me?" Gookmis holds me close and says in her quiet, humble voice, "Because this is what I've been told, by my Grandmother."

Mishkiki *(Mi•sh•ki•ki)* — Medicine

I've been told by my Gookmis that our people lived in harmony with the natural world around us. She taught me to gather mishkiki from the earth to help in our healing.

Mishoomis *(Mish•oh•mis)* — Grandfather

Mishoomis is another special teacher in our lives. He is a provider and a warrior with much knowledge to pass on to the younger generations. Mishoomis knows many teachings. One of them includes the teachings of the fire that he passes down to the young men. Mishoomis says men tend to the fire while everyone learns about caring for fire. I've been told that when you are ready, you will recognize the spirit of fire within you.

Shkode *(Sh•ko•deh)* — Fire

As part of the four elements, fire is an important part of everyone's life. These teachings include preparing the fire, starting the fire, feeding the fire and caring for the people who sit around it. We honour the fire and are grateful for it. Mishoomis has told me we all have a fire within us that needs to be nourished in a good way.

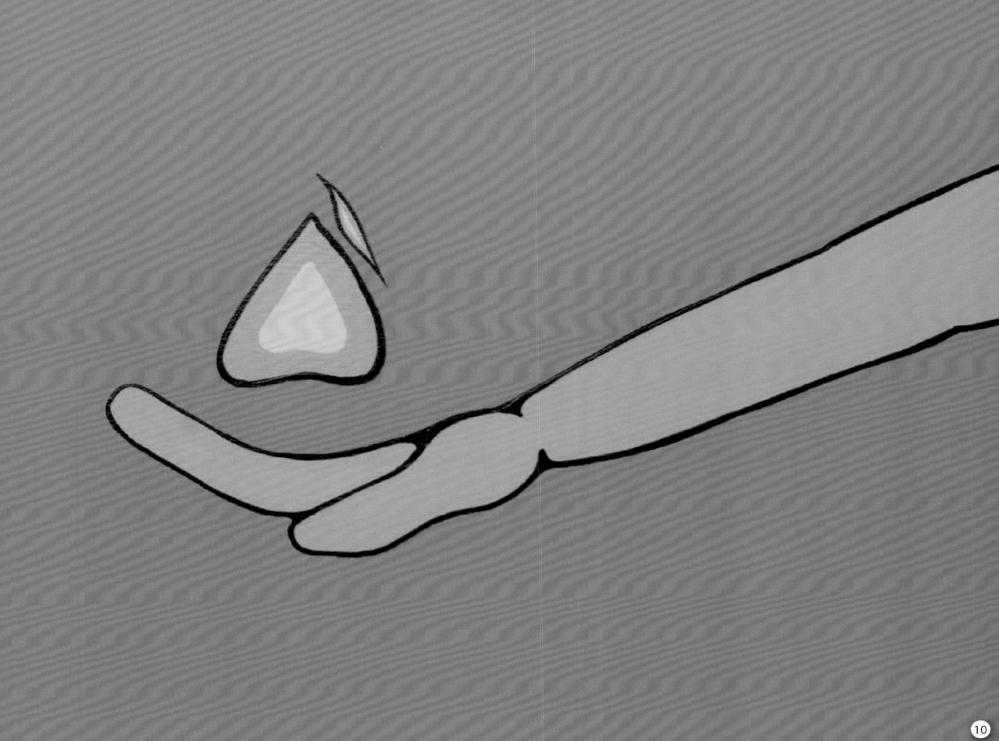

Midewewin *(Mid•eh•we•win)* — Good-Hearted Way

Gookmis and Mishoomis spend a lot of time in the Lodge, learning from the Midewewin people. I've been told by Gookmis that the Midewewin is a group of good-hearted people dedicated to learning and keeping the teachings of our great Creation story alive. Mishoomis says in the Lodge, stories are shared, language is spoken, and teachings are passed on from one generation to the next through sacred ceremony, in a good-hearted way.

Gaan giigdogegon *(Gone geeg•duh•gay•goon)* — Stop Talking

Like many other Indigenous people, the Ojibway people have had to fight to keep their language and culture strong. Gookmis and Mishoomis were forced to attend Residential School when they were little. I've been told this wasn't a nice school, and they weren't allowed to speak their language or practice their cultural traditions.

Anishnaabemowin *(Anish•naw•beh•moe•in)* — An Indigenous Language

Today, our people are working hard to gain back the knowledge and language that was taken from Gookmis and Mishoomis. Second generation language learners are becoming teachers, and communities are gathering knowledge keepers to pass on the teachings. Mishoomis says Indigenous people are resilient, and as long as we are, the Anishnaabemowin language will continue to live strong.

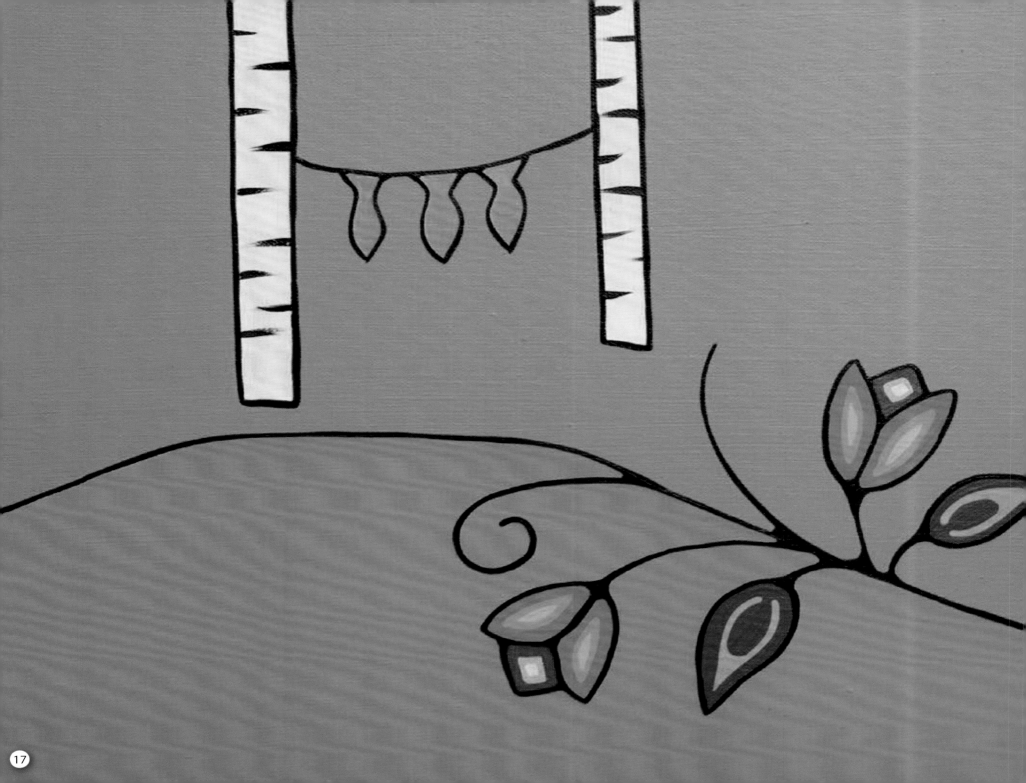

Mno Bimaadziwin *(Mino Bi•mawd•zi•win)* — Living a Good Life

We gather on the land to connect with nature and learn from the natural surroundings. Mno bimaadziwin refers to living a good life. "Gookmis, what is a good life?" Gookmis stops what she's doing and looks deep into the forest. "I've been told a good life is lived in balance with nature and guided by the Seven Grandfather Teachings of our people."

Miigweng kendaaswin *(Meeg•weng ken•daws•win)* — Giving Knowledge

Ojibway people gather in both small and large groups to take care of one another. Sharing their knowledge is a way of survival and a gift they give openly. I've been told that sharing is a way to ensure our culture and language lives from the seven generations before to the next seven generations to come.

Doodem *(Doh•dem)* — Clan

Mishoomis carries the Doodem in the family. He passes it on to the next generation. "Mishoomis, what is a Doodem?" With confidence, Mishoomis answers, "I've been told that a Doodem is the clan animal to which your family follows. Each Doodem has significant skills and meaning in which the families align with and are guided by".

Dewegan *(De•weh•gun)* — Drum

I've been told that the dewegan was a gift from the women during a time of war amongst our men. Today, Mishoomis sits at the dewegan carrying forward the songs of the past and creating new ones for the future. Mishoomis says the dewegan is the heartbeat of our people in times of healing, in ceremony, and in social gathering. It can be heard across Turtle Island, uniting one another in a common journey.

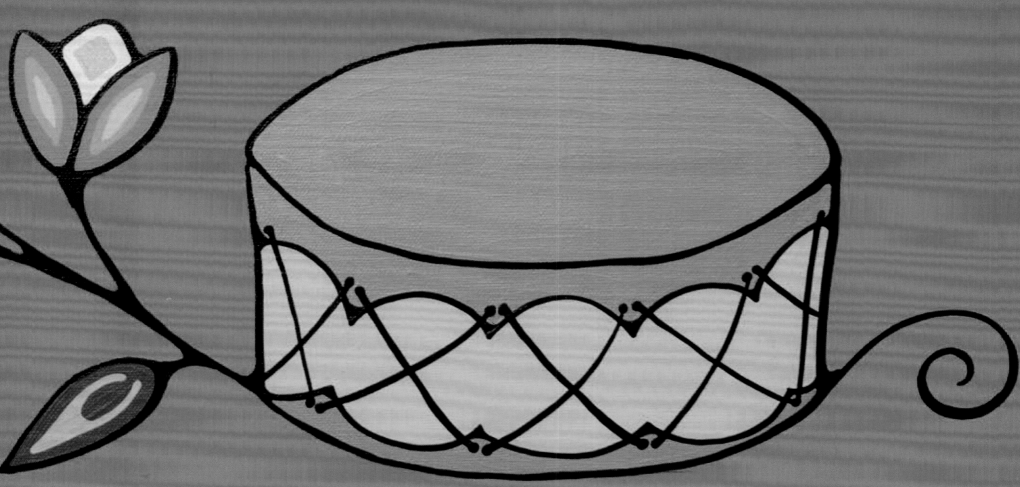

Odemin *(Oh•deh•min)* — Strawberry

Odemin is a sacred gift from the Creator. It is the first berry to arrive after the bear comes out of hibernation. It is a woman's berry. "Gookmis, why is the Odemin a women's berry?" Gookmis says softly, "It represents the heart and the fertility of a woman. The strawberry is a medicine that provides nourishment not only to the bear but also for the women who eat it upon finishing their berry fast. This is what I've been told."

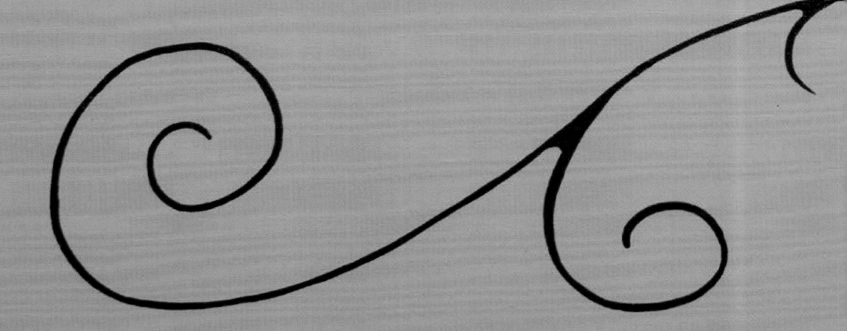

Nsidwinaagaazo *(N•sid•win•aw•gaw•zo)* — Identity

I've been told when all of these teachings are passed down from one generation to the next, good things happen, and our Nsidwinaagaazo remains strong. Language is learned, knowledge is shared, culture is practiced, and mno bimaadziwin happens. Knowing our culture means knowing who we are. When we know who we are, we can walk in a good way.

Ode (Oh·deh) — Heart

My Ode always feels good when I see our people, and others, making an effort to speak our language. Gookmis says she has been told that when you use your mind and your heart equally, you will find balance.

Throughout my life, I will follow in the footsteps of my Gookmis, learning the ways of our people. I will pick the same berries she picked. I will gather the same medicines and flowers she gathered. Speak the same language she spoke to me, and I will carry the Seven Grandfather Teachings she taught me.

When I become a Gookmis, I will carry with me all of the knowledge I need to pass down to the next generation, so they too can live the good life of mno bimaaziwin.

This is what I've been told.

Miigwech *(Meeg•wech)* — Thank You

Miigwech for everything I've been told.

Juliana Armstrong
Ojibway
Nipissing First Nation, Ontario